KT-145-234

Houses
and
Homes

John Williams

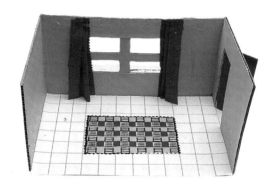

WAYLAND

DESIGN and MAKE

Houses and Homes
Things to Wear
Toys and Games
Wheels and Transport

First published in 1997 by Wayland Publishers Ltd,
61 Western Road, Hove, East Sussex BN3 1JD, England
© Copyright 1997 Wayland Publishers Ltd
Series planned and produced by Margot Richardson

British Library Cataloguing in Publication Data
Williams, John, 1936–
Houses & Homes. - (Design & Make)
1. Dwellings - Models - Juvenile literature
2. House construction - Juvenile literature
3. Architecture, Domestic - Juvenile literature
I. Title
728
ISBN 0 7502 2015 5

Commissioned photography by Zul Mukhida
Designed by Tim Mayer
Edited by Margot Richardson
Equipment supplied by Technology Teaching Systems Ltd, Alfreton, UK
Printed and bound in Italy by G. Canale & C.S.p.A., Turin

CONTENTS

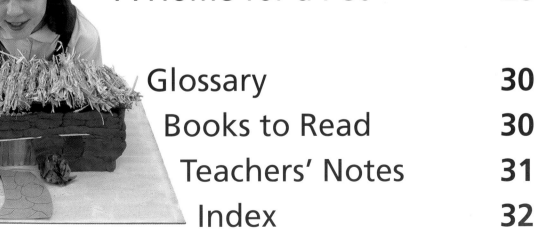

INTRODUCTION

People, all round the world, live in homes of one kind or another. There are many different shapes and types of homes, from small huts to huge blocks of flats. They can be built of all sorts of materials, from straw and mud to glass and steel.

Houses are made to protect us from the weather. Roofs keep the rain off and shade us from hot sun. Walls shelter us from the wind, and also stop water getting in when it rains.

Windows let daylight come in. They can be opened when it is warm and closed when it gets cold. Doors allow us to go in and out, but they too can be shut if it gets windy, wet or cold.

Houses also give us somewhere to put our possessions. We can lock the doors and windows to keep burglars out.

These Greek houses are made from stone and cement. In summer in Greece it can get very hot. To keep the houses cool, they have thick walls and small windows. They are all painted white, to reflect the heat of the sun.

In Indonesia there are plenty of trees, so many houses are made from wood. In this area the rain can be very heavy. The roofs are thick to keep the rain out, and sloped so that the water runs off easily.

Think about the flat or house where you live.

● What are the walls made from? They may be wood, brick or stone – or something else.

● How many rooms does it have? Make a list of all the rooms.

● What sort of roof does it have? Flat or sloping? What is it made from?

● How many outside doors does it have? How many inside, going from room to room?

● How many windows does it have? Is there one in every room?

● Does it have special heating? People in cold countries need heating; people in hot countries might need a way to cool their home.

Write a list, or a story, of how your home is made.

This house in the United States was designed by a famous architect called Frank Lloyd Wright. It is called 'Falling Waters' because it is built on top of a waterfall.

NATIVE AMERICAN TEEPEE

YOU WILL NEED

- Six bamboo poles, approx 1.8m long
- 3m string or cord
- Old sheet or bedspread
- Large paper fasteners
- Paints (optional)
- Paintbrush

Native Americans have lived in North America for thousands of years. Some of them were hunters. They followed herds of buffalo that they killed for their food. Because they were always moving, they needed homes they could take with them. These were teepees, made from animal skins, sewn around long wooden poles. This teepee is made from material, because there are not enough buffaloes to hunt any more.

A teepee is a type of tent, where a covering is held up by a rigid frame. Here is a way to make your own teepee, big enough to go inside.

It is probably easiest to make the teepee outside, on grass if possible. You can push the poles into the ground to keep them firmly in place.

1 Take the bamboo poles and hold them together. Wind the string around them, about 20cm from one end. Tie the string in a knot.

2 Hold the poles upright, with the tied ends at the top. Start to move them out at the bottom to make the shape of a teepee.

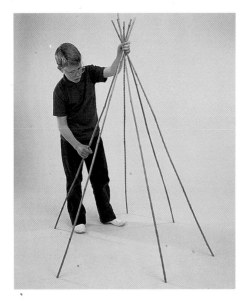

3 Gradually spread the poles to form an even circle at the bottom. Make sure they are firmly anchored on the ground, so that they do not fall over.

4 Take the material and wrap it around the frame. Remember to leave an opening for a door. It may help to use paper fasteners to attach the material to the poles.

5 Native Americans often painted their homes with designs. Decorate your teepee with the paint, and allow it to dry.

NOW TRY THIS

The animal skins used by the Native Americans were thick enough to keep out the wind and rain. You can make your teepee waterproof by adding a big sheet of plastic over the material.

'MUD' HOUSE

Some people are not able to buy wood or bricks to build their houses. They must use whatever they can find around them. All over the world, people use earth or clay to build walls, and straw or branches for a roof. Here is a model house you can build in the same way.

YOU WILL NEED

- Wooden board, painted or covered with plastic to make it waterproof
- Potter's clay or modelling clay
- Lolly sticks
- Straight sticks
- Straw or hay
- Sticky tape

1 Decide on the shape of your house and draw the shape with a pencil on the board. Start to build the walls around the pencil line.

2 Keep building up the walls. They should not be too thin, or they will fall over. Leave gaps for windows and a door.

Homes do not have to look like a square or a rectangle. Many African people build houses in the shape of a circle. These houses in Nigeria are made from earth, and the roofs are covered with straw.

3 To stop the wall above the windows and doors falling down into the space, make a lintel. Put a lolly stick over the top of each gap.

4 Keep building up the walls. The wooden lintels will stop the clay falling into the spaces left for the door and windows.

5 The roof can be flat or sloping. Use long sticks to make a frame across the house to hold up the roof. These are called rafters.

6 Use the straw or hay to make a roof. It may help to tie it in bundles first, using sticky tape. Make some bundles and lie them across the rafters.

DESIGN A HOME

YOU WILL NEED

- Large sheets of squared or graph paper
- Pencil
- Ruler
- Rubber
- Felt-tip pens (optional)

Imagine you are going to design a new flat or house. Let's decide that it will have two bedrooms, a kitchen, a living room and a bathroom.

When you are doing this, it may help to think about your own home, and how its rooms are arranged.

1 Make a list of the things to put in your house. You will have to include doors and windows. Don't forget that every home needs a front door as well.

2 Draw your design on the squared paper. First, mark out the rooms. Will there be a hallway, with all the rooms coming off it? Or will most rooms open off the main room?

People who design buildings are called architects. They talk to the people who are paying for the building, to find out what they want. Then they draw plans to show what the place will look like. When it is being built, the architect checks that the builder is doing it correctly.

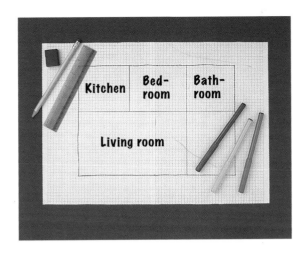

3 On the plan, write down the name of each room, for example Bedroom, Kitchen, etc.

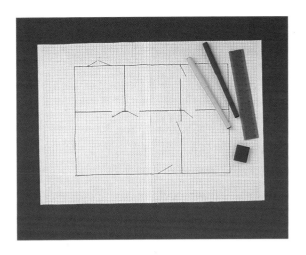

4 Decide where the doors will go. Each room needs a door, and some rooms may have more than one.

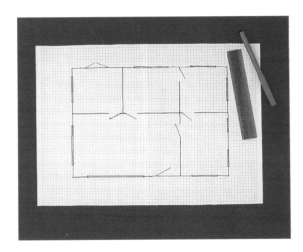

5 Then mark where the windows will go, on the outside wall of the house. Each room should have at least one window.

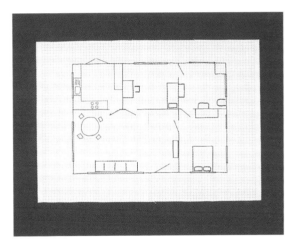

6 If you wish, you can even mark where the furniture would go. Draw the shapes of things such as tables, chairs, beds and cupboards.

NOW TRY THIS

Draw a real plan, like a map, of a room in your home. It could be your bedroom, or perhaps the living room. Draw it so that 1 metre in the room equals 1cm on your plan. To do this you will need a long ruler or a tape measure to measure everything in the room.

MODEL ROOM

When a home has been designed and planned (see pages 10–11), it can then be built. Here are ideas for making a model room, with windows and doors.

A model like this is easy to glue with PVA if the glue is put on, then allowed to dry a little before pushing the pieces together.

YOU WILL NEED

- Stiff cardboard for base
- Thick, soft cardboard for walls
- Thin see-through plastic for windows
- PVA glue
- Scraps of fabric
- Pencil
- Ruler
- Scissors
- Sticky or masking tape
- Paint and paintbrush

1 Find a piece of stiff card. Using a pencil and ruler, mark out the size and shape of the room you are going to make.

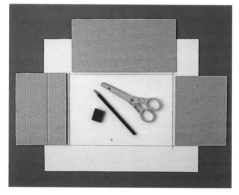

2 Measure the length of each wall on your plan, and cut them out of thick card. Each wall should be about 12cm high.

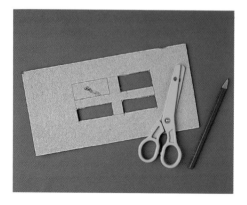

3 Draw the shapes of the windows on the walls. Cut them out. Cut a piece of thin plastic to cover the window.

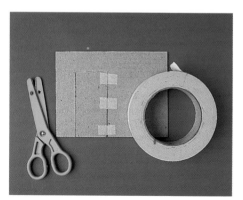

4 Cut a door shape in a wall. Make hinges out of sticky or masking tape, and join the door to the wall down one side.

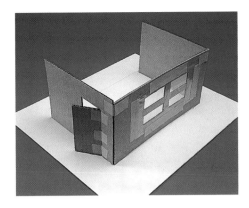

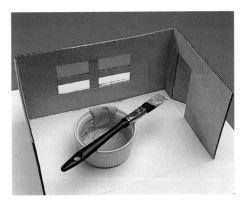

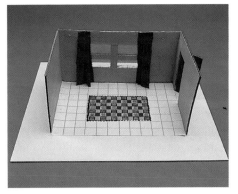

5 Stick the walls along the lines you drew in step 1. Use small pieces of tape on the outside to hold the corners together, if needed.

6 When the glue holding the walls together has dried, paint the insides of the walls, the window and the door, so they look as real as possible.

7 You may wish to add scraps of fabric for curtains. You could also paint the floor to look like wood, or cover it with felt, to look like carpet.

Architects and builders often make models of buildings they are going to build. They make the models look as real as possible, with gardens, trees, cars and even model people. This helps everyone to see what the building will look like when it is finished.

NOW TRY THIS

If you enjoyed making this room, you could try making a whole home, with several different rooms. It could be based on the design for a home – see pages 10–11. Or you could make a model of your own home.

ELECTRICITY AT HOME

The amount of electricity that comes into homes is very strong and can be dangerous if not used properly. However, here are ways to learn about electricity, using small batteries and light bulbs that cannot harm you.

YOU WILL NEED

- Battery (4.5V minimum)
- Bulbs (3.5V minimum)
- Bulb holders
- Single-core electrical wire
- Wire strippers and cutters
- Small piece of card
- Scissors
- Paper fasteners

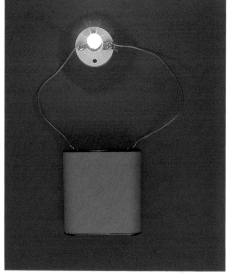

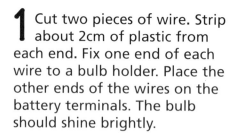

1 Cut two pieces of wire. Strip about 2cm of plastic from each end. Fix one end of each wire to a bulb holder. Place the other ends of the wires on the battery terminals. The bulb should shine brightly.

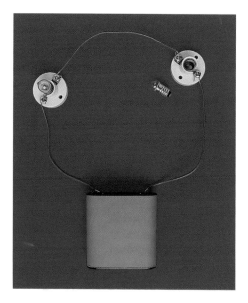

2 Cut another length of wire so that you can include another bulb in the circuit. Do both the bulbs shine? Are they both as bright as the single bulb? Unscrew one bulb. What happens to the other one?

Electricity can be very dangerous if it is not used properly.
- **Never play with electric sockets**
- **Do not touch or use bare wires**
- **Never use electricity with wet or damp hands.**

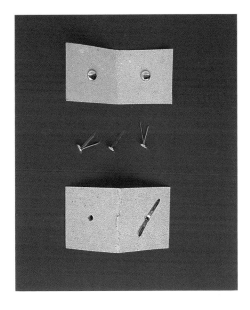 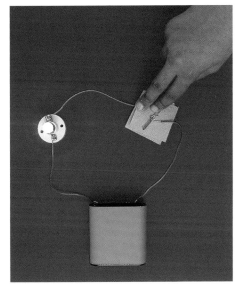 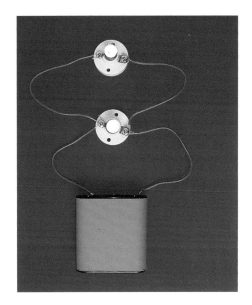

3 Make a switch for the circuit. Cut a small piece of card, about 5 x 2cm. Make a small hole in each half of the card. Put a paper fastener in each hole with the points on the outside.

4 Twist the bare ends of the wires round the pointed ends of the paper fasteners. Close the switch. The round tops of the paper fasteners should touch, and the bulb should light up. This is called a series circuit.

5 This photo shows a different type of circuit. Put this together with two bulbs. How bright are all the bulbs? Unscrew one bulb. What happens to the others? This is called a parallel circuit.

Most modern homes have electricity in all the rooms. It gives us power for many different things, such as lights, television, stereos, and cooking. People who do not have electricity cannot use all these things, and they may have to light their homes at night with oil lamps.

NOW TRY THIS

Lights in homes are made up of parallel circuits. You can put lights in your model room using the small bulbs and a battery.

MODEL FURNITURE

Furniture makes homes more comfortable. We use chairs to sit on, tables to put things on, cupboards to keep things in. Without furniture we would have to sit, eat and sleep on the ground.

Here is a way to make a model table. Once you have finished it, you can go on to make a whole range of models to go with it.

YOU WILL NEED

- 60cm wood, approx 1 x 1cm square
- Thick cardboard
- PVA glue
- Pencil
- Ruler
- Hacksaw
- Paint and paintbrush

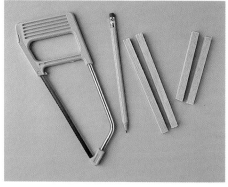

1 Decide on the shape and size of your table. Measure and cut four pieces of wood for the frame of the table's top.

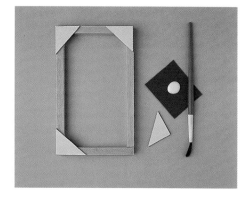

2 Glue the pieces of wood together. It may help to use cardboard triangles to get the corners exactly square.

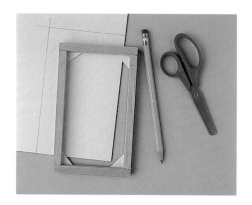

3 When the glue has dried, use the frame to mark out a piece of card for the table top. Cut it out and glue it on.

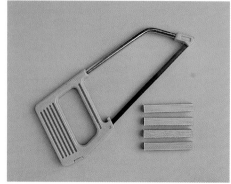

4 Decide how high you want your table to be. Measure this height, and cut four equal pieces of wood for the legs.

Dolls houses have been made for hundreds of years. Some were just for children to play with. Others were like works of art with beautiful rooms and dolls. They had furniture which was made exactly like the real thing, only much smaller.

NOW TRY THIS

Now you know how to cut and join lengths of wood, try making another item of furniture such as a chair to go with the table, or a bed, or a cupboard. Look at real pieces of furniture to see how they are made, and copy them.

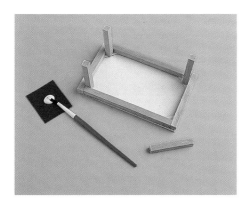

5 Put some glue on the top of each leg, and round each inside corner of the frame. Let it dry a little and put each leg in place.

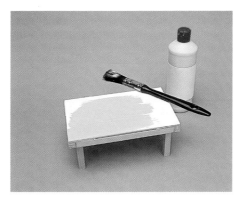

6 Paint the table so that it is the same colour all over. It could be a bright colour, or you could make it look as though it is all made from wood.

SOLAR WATER HEATER

Around the world, some homes have hot water, ready to use at any time. It is usually heated by a boiler, using electricity, gas, oil or coal. But the sun can make water hot, too.

YOU WILL NEED

- Lid of a cardboard box
- Clear PVC tubing, about 8mm diameter
- Aluminium kitchen foil
- Thin wire (such as single-core electric wire)
- Clear plastic (to cover the lid)
- Sticky tape
- Small plastic funnel
- Plastic modelling clay (eg Plasticine)

1 Take the aluminium foil and line the box lid, covering its bottom and sides. Fix the foil with sticky tape, if needed.

2 Measure the box, and work out how much tube you will need for it to go up and down the box a few times.

3 Fix the tube into the box. Use small pieces of wire that go through the cardboard and tie round the tube. Make holes at either end for the tube to pass out of the box. Cover the box with clear plastic. Hold it down at the sides with sticky tape.

4 Put a small ball of modelling clay over the lower end of the tube, to keep the water in. Fill the tube with water, using a funnel. Put another ball of clay over the top end of the tube. Wait for a sunny day and put the box in a window.

5 At the end of the day, take the box out of the window. Take the stopper off the ends of the tube and let the water run out. Test the water to see if it is warm.

Solar water heaters have panels to catch the heat of the sun. The panels can be put on roofs, or on the ground. The sun's energy heats water, which is used for washing and heating. Solar power is used all over the world. This system is for a hotel in the Himalayan mountains.

BUILDING A ROOF

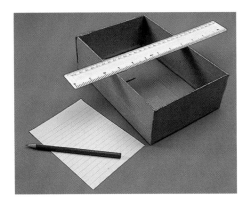

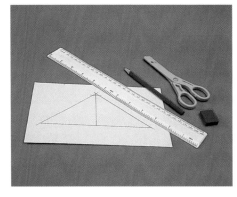

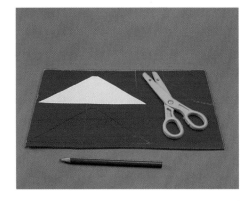

1 Measure across the box. Add on about 2cm to this length so that the roof will hang over the edge on either side. Decide on the height of the roof.

2 Draw a triangle on paper. The bottom will be the length worked out in step 1. Draw a line to cut off the top point. Cut out the paper shape.

3 Use the paper triangle as a template. Mark the shape on the plastic and cut it out. You will need at least four triangles to hold up the roof.

Most buildings have roofs that slope. The angle of the roof helps rain run off, to keep it out of the house. A roof shape that looks like an upside-down V is called a pitched roof.

YOU WILL NEED

- Small cardboard box
- Plastic corrugated sheet (or thick cardboard)
- Cardboard (for roof)
- PVA glue
- Pencil
- Ruler
- Scissors
- Paint and paintbrush (optional)

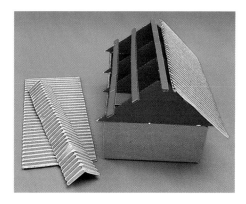

4 Glue the triangles to the top of the box. It will be easiest if you put the glue on, let it dry a little, then stick the pieces together.

5 You need to add rafters to hold the triangles together and support the roof. Measure the length and cut long pieces of plastic. Glue them in place.

6 Add the roof itself. Cut two pieces of card, one for each side. Then cut a V-shaped piece to go over the top. Glue them on, and paint them if you wish.

When a house is being built, the walls are put up first. Then the roof is added. Usually, the roof must have a framework to hold it up. When the frame has been made, it can be covered with tiles, stone (such as slate), sheets of metal, wood, or even straw.

INUIT IGLOO

The Inuit (also known as Eskimos) live in the freezing, snow-covered parts of Alaska and Canada. Many years ago, they made their homes from blocks of ice – the only material they could find to build with. Here you can learn how the Inuit built their houses. We use sugar cubes instead of ice, and cotton wool instead of snow.

YOU WILL NEED

- Stiff cardboard for base
- Round lid, for drawing a circle
- Pencil
- Box of sugar cubes
- PVA glue
- Cotton wool
- Pebbles and gravel (optional)

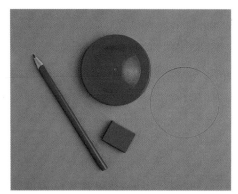

1 Using the round lid and a pencil, draw a circle on the baseboard. This gives you a size and shape to build the igloo.

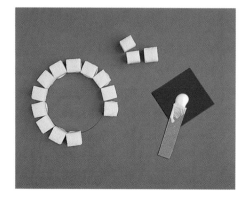

2 Put a little glue on one side of each cube, and place them round the circle. Leave a gap for the door.

3 When a circle is finished, stick another on top. Make each circle smaller than the last, to build a dome shape.

NOW TRY THIS

Use sugar cubes to build other models. They could be used like bricks to make walls, or laid flat on the ground like paving stones.

An Inuit man cuts blocks of ice with a long knife. The ice can be cut to make a neat curved shape. When the blocks are all put together, any small holes are filled with smaller pieces of ice, or snow. This helps to keep the wind out.

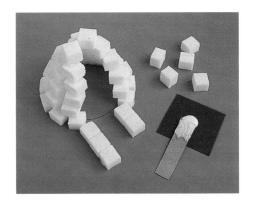

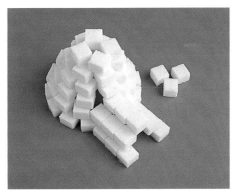

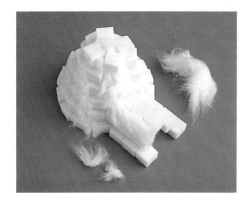

4 When the dome is finished, except for the door space, start to build the tunnel at the front of the igloo.

5 Finish the tunnel. Close the gap above it by gluing on more sugar cubes wherever they are necessary.

6 Although the igloo shape has now been built, it has many holes between the cubes. Fill these up with cotton wool.

ARMCHAIR

YOU WILL NEED

- Large amounts of old newspaper
- Old cartons made from thick cardboard
- Strong parcel/packing tape
- Scissors
- Material for covering chair
- Dressmaker's or safety pins

Most chairs and tables are designed for adults to sit in. A grown-up's chair can be uncomfortable for a child, so here is a way of making a custom-built chair – just for you.

1 Make the seat of the chair from newspaper. Pile up lots of folded papers until you have made a height that is comfortable to sit on. Bind the papers together with parcel tape.

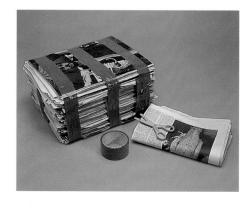

2 Make the back of the chair from thick, stiff cardboard. Cut a piece that is high enough to support your back. Join it to the seat with more tape, making the joins as strong as possible.

Most furniture is made to be as useful as as possible. This means that it should be hard to break, easy to clean and comfortable to use. However, furniture can be interesting to look at, and even fun as well.

NOW TRY THIS

What did you notice about the rolls of paper you made for the arms? When held together tightly with tape, they are very strong. Think of other things you could design and make, using rolled recycled paper and thick cardboard.

3 Cut lengths of newspaper the same depth as the seat from front to back. Roll them tightly into a tube, and fix them with tape. Join the tubes to the seat to make arms for the chair.

4 Cover the finished chair with some material. Pin it in place, if necessary, to cover the chair properly.

MINIATURE GARDEN

A beautiful garden should be designed as carefully as the inside of a house. Think of all the things you would like to have in a garden. You might want grass to play on, a tree to climb or a swing. You could also have a barbecue, a vegetable patch or a pond.

YOU WILL NEED

- Shallow plastic tray, such as a seed tray
- Sand or gravel
- Flexible garden wire
- Lolly sticks
- Scraps of cardboard
- Wood glue
- Tissue paper
- Green felt
- 20 x 20cm piece of black plastic
- Small pebbles
- Plastic modelling clay (eg Plasticine)

1 Fill the plastic tray with sand or small pieces of gravel, almost to the top. Pack it down, and smooth it so that lies quite flat.

2 Use wooden twigs, pieces of card, wire, tissue paper, fabric, paint and modelling clay to make trees, bushes, leaves and flowers.

3 Make items such as a fence, bench, swing, wooden 'deck' and garden arch from wooden lolly sticks, card, string and wire.

4 Use a piece of green felt to look like grass. Cut it to fit, and lie it over the gravel. Cut small holes in it to plant trees and flowers.

Gardens can be used to grow flowers or vegetables, or to play in. Some people have very small gardens, just big enough to sit in. Grand houses used to have huge decorative gardens. These needed many people working in them all the time to keep them looking good.

6 Arrange all the things you have made in the garden. Make more plants from tissue paper and paint on flowers. Fill the pond with a little water.

5 You may wish to add a garden pond. Make a hole in the gravel or sand, line it with black plastic. Hold the plastic down with pebbles all round.

A HOME FOR A PET

YOU WILL NEED

- Plain paper
- Pencil
- Rubber

Animals also have homes. Some live in holes in the ground, others make nests. Animals who are tame and live with us are called pets. Just like us, they need somewhere warm to sleep at night, food, drink, and things to exercise and play with.

Imagine you had to design a home for a hamster. Hamsters are small animals. They cannot run round our homes like a cat or a dog, or they would get lost or injured. They need a safe home of their own.

Hamsters like somewhere cosy to sleep, such as a box filled with hay or a soft nest.

Hamsters have very strong front teeth. They can gnaw through anything except thick glass, plastic or metal, so their home must be made from one of these materials. It should be lined with sawdust to make it comfortable.

Pigs on farms are happiest when they can live outdoors. As well as being fed by the farmer, they look for things to eat in the ground. The farmer also makes sure they have a house for shelter when the weather is bad, and for sleeping.

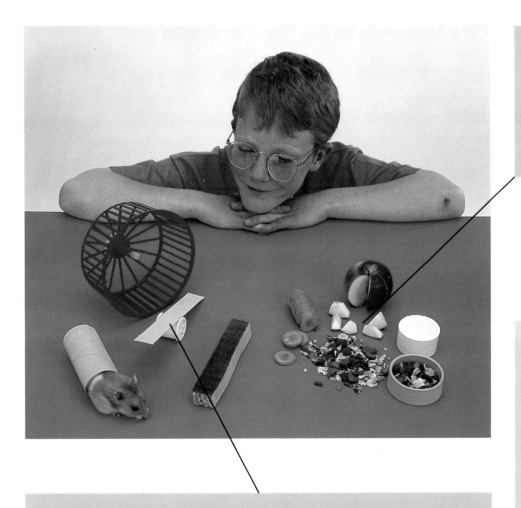

Like all living things, hamsters have to eat and drink. Hamsters like to eat dry seeds and pellets, and fresh food such as apple and carrot.

Now that you know all about how to keep a hamster, draw a picture of an ideal home. It will need separate areas for sleeping, going to the toilet, eating and drinking, and playing. Like people's houses, it could be on more than one storey, with ladders linking them.

Hamsters like things to do and places to explore. Every hamster should have an exercise wheel, and will also use things like ramps, ladders, branches, jam jars, cardboard tubes and cotton reels.

GLOSSARY

architect	A person who designs buildings.
boiler	A machine for heating water.
circuit	An arrangement of things through which an electric current passes.
cube	A shape that has six sides that are all square and the same size.
designing	Getting an idea, planning and sometimes making a drawing.
dome	A shape that looks like ball cut in half.
frame	A strong shape that can hold up things put over the top of it.
gnaw	To bite and chew.
hinge	A joint that moves, letting things like doors and windows open and close.
lining	Putting a layer of something inside something else, such as inside a box or hole.
lintel	A piece of wood or stone placed over a door or window to support the wall above.
materials	Things that are used for making and building, such as wood, cement, bricks, glass, fabrics, etc.
miniature	Something that is much smaller than normal.
model	An object made to look like something that is bigger.
pitched (roof)	A roof shape that looks like an upside-down V.
rafter	A piece of wood that forms the frame for a roof.
rigid	Something that is stiff and hard, which will not bend.
solar	Something that uses the sun.
storeys	Levels or floors of a building. A house might have two storeys, for example.
switch	Something that makes and breaks a join in an electric circuit.
template	A shape used to draw around and cut out a number of the same shapes.
tunnel	A long hole, like a tube.
volt (V)	A measurement of the 'push', or force, of electricity.
waterproof	Something that will not let water pass through it, such as plastic or glass.

BOOKS TO READ

Energy: Power from the Sun by Sue Hadden, Wayland, 1993

Exploring Materials: Materials in your Home by Malcolm Dixon, Wayland, 1993

Eyewitness Guides: Building by Philip Wilkinson, Dorling Kindersley, 1995

Homes in Hot and Cold Places by Simon Chrisp, Wayland, 1994

Make it Work!: Electricity by Alexandra Parsons, Two-Can, 1992

My Pet: Hamster by Nigel Taylor, Wayland, 1993

My First Garden Book by Angela Wilkes, Dorling Kindersley, 1992

Peoples Under Threat: Inuit by Helen Edmunds, Wayland, 1995

Peoples Under Threat: Native Americans by Helen Edmunds, Wayland, 1995

TEACHERS' NOTES

Design Technology starts with a simple idea, and then by stages of research, development and testing, ends with a fully evaluated final product. Although this is a process which can be undertaken by professional adults, it may not be suitable for children who have yet to develop the concept of design, and have had little experience of the materials needed to make working models and artefacts. However, the topic of Houses and Homes gives children plenty of opportunity for design. They will all have first-hand knowledge of their own homes, and this can be used as foundation on which to develop their ideas.

Native American Teepee, 'Mud' House and Inuit Igloo

These three houses are examples of how to make the best use of the materials available. A traditional teepee, although easily carried about, was very strong when erected. A longer pole was put at the back of the teepee to face the prevailing wind, and two flaps could be opened at the top to let out the smoke of the fire. The mud and ice used for the two other houses represent the extremes of the climate that exist in these areas. Children may not always be able to use these exact materials, but nevertheless these projects give them the opportunity to develop their technological skills, experiment with a range of structures, and provide cross-curricular topics for linking into geography and other cultures.

Design a Home
It is often difficult for children to design structures or models without first having experience of the materials with which they would need to build. However, they all know what houses are, and should therefore be able to make good designs. They should be allowed as much freedom as possible to make imaginative designs, but at the same time be encouraged to be precise and accurate, and where possible work to a scale. They can even consider how they would decorate their house by thinking about colour schemes and designs for wallpaper.

Model Room
Again, a good opportunity for freedom of design. Children should be encouraged to keep their designs simple as they will form the base for their models. Because the card should be as rigid as possible, young children may need help with the cutting and sticking. Making scale models is often part of the process from the drawing board to the finished product. At a later stage, children should be allowed to experiment with some of the materials used in building, perhaps as part of their science lessons.

Electricity at Home
Children should be allowed to experiment with bulbs and batteries. They should be encouraged to discover what part of the bulb lights up, and how the electricity seems to flow from one battery terminal to the other. Children need to be made aware of the dangers of electricity, and this project could also give them the opportunity to design suitable posters about this, as well as the importance of saving energy in the home and at school.

Model Furniture
Although this design is being used to make a model table, this basic structure can also be a part of many other technological projects. The combination of square section wood and cardboard corners will form a very rigid structure to make buildings, towers and bridges. It can even be fitted with wheels to make a variety of vehicles.

Building a Roof
Supports for a pitched roof would normally be a hollow structure. One of the problems with a triangular structure of this kind is that over the years the weight of the roof will gradually widen the base of the triangle. Children should be encouraged to understand these 'real life' problems. If some lightweight material could be used in a similar design as this model, then perhaps problems such as these could be overcome.

Solar Water Heater
When investigating the water system children should be made aware that solar heating is an important secondary source of energy which requires no destruction of primary resources such as coal, gas or oil.

Armchair
This project will enable children to carry out a simple ergonomic study. This looks at how people relate to their working environment, and how conditions can be adapted to fit the individual to obtain the maximum efficiency. Children should be encouraged to think about how a chair should not only look good, but should support the body with the minimum of stress and the maximum of comfort. They should analyse the finished product under four headings: comfort, appearance, stability, and safety.

Miniature Garden, Home for a Pet
These projects help to develop the concept of a home beyond the confines of four walls and a roof. It gives plenty of scope for designing, and to use a variety of materials in an imaginative way.

INDEX

Acknowledgements

The author and publishers wish to thank the following for their kind assistance with this book:
models Abdullah Crawford, Josie Kearns, Hugh Williams, Juliet Williams, Yasmin Mukhida and Rebecca
Thomas. Also A. Coombes (Pet Supplies, Brighton), Sylph Baier, Cathy Baxter and
Gus Ferguson.

For the use of their library photographs, grateful thanks are due to:
Bryan and Cherry Alexander p23; Chapel Studios p17 (Graham Horner), p27 (Tim Richardson); Eye
Ubiquitous p10 (K. Wilton), p29 (Paul Seheult); Photri Inc p5 (Tracy Wetherby), p6 (John Robert
McCauley), p13 (Richard Nowitz), p21; Topham Picturepoint pp 5 & 25. All other photographs belong to
the Wayland Picture Library.